I0648470

Aella Greene

After Night

A Summerplace Talk, With Other Poems

Aella Greene

After Night
A Summerplace Talk, With Other Poems

ISBN/EAN: 9783744705493

Printed in Europe, USA, Canada, Australia, Japan

Cover: Foto ©Thomas Meinert / pixelio.de

More available books at **www.hansebooks.com**

AFTER NIGHT,

A SUMMER-PLACE TALK,

WITH

OTHER POEMS.

BY

AELLA GREENE,

AUTHOR OF "'RHYMES OF YANKEE LAND," AND "HAPPY DAYS AT HAMPTON."

———•♦•———

BOSTON:

LEE & SHEPARD.

NEW YORK:

LEE, SHEPARD & DILLINGHAM.

1873.

Entered according to Act of Congress, in the year 1873, by
A E L L A   G R E E N E,
In the Office of the Librarian of Congress at Washington.

CLARK W. BRYAN & COMPANY,
ELECTROTYPERS, PRINTERS AND BINDERS,
SPRINGFIELD, MASS.

TO

Hon. Henry L. Dawes,

IN REMEMBRANCE OF HIS INSPIRING AND SINCERE
WORDS OF KINDNESS,

I Dedicate

"AFTER NIGHT."

CONTENTS.

CONTENTS.

AFTER NIGHT.

"WHERE WE HAVE COME TO SUMMER."

WHERE we have come to summer
 Refreshing breezes blow,
The meads are decked with flowers,
 The streamlets murmur low.
The mountains are around us,
 Their tops against the sky,
The mountains bold, majestic,
 That give us notions high.

Although we think of heaven,
 These scenes have greatest worth,
In that they make us happy
 In dwelling on the earth;
And willing, while we tarry,

To labor for mankind,

And careful climb life's ladder,

Our final good to find.

The village is a model

Of neatness and of thrift,

And everything within it

Is on the upward drift.

The cottages are painted

In trim, becoming style;

We have choice, cosy quarters,

We better stop awhile.

In search for health and comfort,

I think we've planned it well,

To sojourn at the "Mansion,"

Pas'comuck's good hotel,

Where pleasant people tarry,
  Away from "Saratogue,"
And all the rounds of fashion
  Among "the ton" in vogue.

The ladies are conversing
  As their bright minds incline,
Those two delightful women,
  Your wife, dear James, and mine.
They're happy in the parlor,
  And hark! a song they sing,
A grand old anthem, bravely,
  To tune of royal ring.

And here ensconced together,
  We'll cast our vision back
The path we traveled hither,

And trace the devious track;

And see through all our journey

Day coming after night;

If thorns, yet still the roses,

And all things working right.

I readily remember

Yours was a sadder sky;

The angel me protecting

Appeared to pass you by.

And still you had some blessings,

Resembling choicest gold;

Some days with joys were crowded,

As full as days could hold.

"YOU WROTE ME FROM THE CITY."

YOU wrote me from the city
   That you were sad at heart,
And thought that I might reckon
   That grieving is your art.
But, James, have done with sorrow;
   There's reason to be glad,
Besides the many reasons
   That ceaseless sorrow's bad.

'Tis good, friend James, to see you,
   And take your hearty hand,
And see, in spite of sorrow,
   You 're looking glad and bland.
That you may have the courage

To fight life's battle through,
   You should be still more joyful.
And there's more joy for you.

And I will entertain you,
   If you will give me leave,
That through this happy morning
   You have no time to grieve;
Will speak of your good blessings,
   Predicting you some more,
Your brightest days repeated
   In future o'er and o'er.

We'll bid good-by to business,
   Our business be to rest;
And that, like other callings,
   We'll follow with good zest.

When rest is well accomplished

Ours be some other work;

And so, throughout our life-time,

There be no grain of shirk.

2

OFT hence we'll make excursions
   To Berkshire's breezy hills,
And listen to the music
   Arising from the rills;
We'll gaze on Greylock's grandeur,
   And Housatonic's vale,
For scenes of choicest beauty,
   Was never known to fail;

While memories of giants,
   Like Hopkins, Briggs and Dawes,
Shall teach to work and suffer
   In every noble cause;
And, rambling 'round the mountains,

Perhaps we'll come in sight
Of that delightful village   '
  Where you first saw the light;

Where yours was pleasant study
  When August waned to fall,
Which half the day was summer,
  Or whether autumn all;
When harvest was completed,
  Blackberries decked the hill,
And oxen shed their tackle
  And browsed the lot at will;

When trees were bent with sweetings
  Around a buckwheat field,
Affording fragrant promise
  Of an abundant yield;

And you believed that heaven

   Was through the upper blue,

And thought the good departed

   No happier than you!

So, in our Berkshire rambles,

   We'll plan to come in sight

Of that delightful village

   Where you first saw the light;

And where you passed your childhood

   And had your griefs and joys,

In much the same proportion

   As did the other boys;

And where, a little later,

   Your trouble did begin;

And you had sore departed

To foolishness and sin,
Because some people doubted
  Who should have given trust,
And all your pleasant castles
  Were crumbled into dust!

And so my words sound strangely
  That call the village blest,
Though there you 'gan your being,
  And there your kindred rest!
And yet, you make exception
  About a single case,
Apparently sufficient
  To save the wretched place.

To all your words of trouble
  One gave a full belief;

By faith's refreshing sunshine

  Dispelled your clouds of grief.

He praised you for ambition,

  Your new made plans indorsed,

And helped into his saddle

  Whom cruel men unhorsed. .

"AS WE BELIEVE HIM."

THE project you remember well,
　　When rested with one man
To lift to life, or crush to death,
　　A dearly cherished plan;

A plan to write and bless the world,
　　And win enough of gold,
To purchase books and bread and clothes,
　　And shelter from the cold.

This enterprise appeared to some
　　Assumption on your part;
They charged you with a foolish pride
　　And vanity of heart.

Some angel then directed you

    To dwelling of the squire,

Whose kingly soul beamed from his eyes,

    As, at his parlor fire,

He greeted you with cheerful word

    And half divined your plan ;

And, in a world of little men,

    You found one noble man !

He heard your story, read you through,

    And rose unto his feet,

And spoke the words I've often heard

    You joyfully repeat :

" You ask me here to recognize

    That you are fit to do

The noble work you truly think
　　You are adapted to.

"And that I will, most heartily,
　　And patronize you well;
How high your enterprise may run
　　No one can fully tell.

"My social sanction, hard-earned cash,
　　And prayers that God will bless,
I give you, with my sincere faith,
　　Predicting you success.

"But little in my power to do,
　　I do it with my heart;
As you begin your long life-race,
　　I'm proud to see you start!"

Heart-felt adieus were interchanged,
And, grateful, glad and strong,
You left that Bethel of your life,
Your heart uplift with song.

The squire, for prudence noted far,
Was queried much by some,
Who thought this extra charity
Had best "begin to hum."

"And he should pay the minister,
Or paint the old town hall,
Or prop his neighbors' fences up,
That were about to fall."

And that to one whose very life
Was given to the town;

Whose quickest instinct was to lift

A fellow fallen down!

One cautious neighbor, doubting, asked,

"Why show such faith as this?"

And quick the squire replied with force,

"Therein I have my bliss.

"To see this man is bound to win

It needs no prophet's ken;

The gospel will be understood

When men believe in men.

"*As we believe him he will be;*

If we doubt, he will fall;

And let us, while we're trusting him,

Largely trust, trust him all.

"No measured kindness should be shown,
　　Nor artificial cheer ;
　Much we should trust him, always bless,
　　And hold his interests dear.

"God pity those who can't believe
　　Unless they see the end !
　According to the Scriptures, man,
　　Where do such notions tend ?

"Excuse me, sir, if thus I hint
　　Such doubting smacks of hell !
　But is not that where doubters go,
　　As Bible teachings tell ?

"Fay though you are, you act the fiend !
　　You laugh at this kind deed ?

Why, disbelieving, selfish man,
    I'd help e'en you in need!

"But, by my word, you damage more,
    In any way, this man,
Whom and whose parents you esteem
    But worthy social ban,

"Depend on most unhappy luck
    In all you hope or do;
And count on rugged hills and thorns
    Your whole hard journey through!"

This Fay, I think, soon after died,
    And six paid mourners wept,
And two pale poplars marked the spot
    Wherein his ashes slept.

The squire, perennial like the streams
That sing his vale along,
Is brighter with advancing years,
And with his age grows strong.

"WHERE BRIGHT A RIVER'S CRYSTAL TIDE."

"WHERE BRIGHT A RIVER'S CRYSTAL TIDE."

WHERE bright a river's crystal tide
  Descends a steep cascade,
To drive a dozen toiling mills,
  Where useful goods are made,

There is another village blest
  With men of enterprise,
Whose peaceful lives, 'twixt wealth and want,
  And happy social skies,

And lively interest in things
  Of church and neighborhood,
And constant watchfulness for ways
  To do each other good,

3

Might well be envied by a king,

And prompt with better ken,

To sing the happiness and worth

Of these great-hearted men.

And trustful there, but trembling still,

You asked for blessings small;

The noble answer ne'er shall pass

Beyond your memory's call;

Nor pass from mind the happy hours

Beneath the pleasant shade

Of quiet streets, where cosy homes

An Eden picture made!

And walking there, you planned to build

Your work so sure and strong,

It should remain to bless the earth,
  A good enduring long.

Forever shall be dear to you
  The cordial greeting said
By one whose kindness was so wise,
  Yet free, your heart was led

To banish doubts and live by faith,
  By trust in royal souls;
By faith that watchful Providence,
  Who all the world controls,

And strangely doth, at times, permit
  Some littleness in earth,
Hath, yet, some royal contrasts made,
  In men whose ways and worth

Resemble characters the bards

   To ransomed ones have given,   .

And which, did all possess, would make

   This earth completest heaven.

Unto this man each useful craft

   Appeared a noble trade;

No honest calling, well pursued,

   Did in his eyes degrade.

His daily business was to drive

   The works where plows were made;

And in his creed and daily walk

   Great stress on smiles was laid.

His gracious presence often cheered

   The Hampden harvest club,

And gave right tone to General Court,
　　Assembled at the "Hub."

For years he led the Sunday-school
　　With dignity and grace;
Nor stories told to prompt the boys
　　To learn as on a race.

Hard by his house the village church,
　　The happy Sabbath home,
Where lovers of the good old way
　　Took great delight to come.

And you and I, one Sabbath day,
　　Chanced in that house of God;
And reverently, with peace and joy,
　　Those pleasant aisles we trod.

We heard the pastor preach the truth
  Of every sham bereft;
Before him earnest Christians sat,
  And, at the preacher's left,

The sweet-voiced organ and the choir,
  Whose faces beamed with song,
Whose notes of praise, so "glad and free,"
  Shall linger with me long!

And to the young men's class at noon
  The village judge discoursed,
As fittingly on Scripture texts,
  And moral truths enforced,

As he the common law explained
  To sinners 'gainst the law;

And from a field of wide research
    Did useful lessons draw.

· The sun was setting as we walked
    Along the shaded street,
And through an opening in the trees
    Beheld a vision sweet!

The pleasant river winding bright
    A circling ridge around,
And whispering pines and graceful elms
    The little mountain crowned.

And still beyond a verdant plain
    Where erst the Indians were,
Before these lands were bought by whites
    For beads, ear-rings, and fur.

And down the river, just descried,
   Great factories arose,
Where short the river's lesser tide
   Within a grander flows!

And farther up the silver stream
   The Indian Orchard place,
Where mills are run and schools are taught
   With industry and grace.

And where the Indians took the leap,
   In fabled days of old,
Into the stream, o'er which, ere long,
   Shall railway trains be rolled,

Connecting Pynchon's ancient town,
   Now smart, ambitious, wise,

With towns, and lakes, and forests, where
  New Hampshire's mountains rise.

Along this stream, above "the leap,"
  A pleasant roadway runs,
On which so happy once I walked
  In best of April suns.

With me a toiling, sickened, man,
  Whose wise, refreshing talk,
Gave thoughts, as though with gods and kings!
  I had this pleasant walk.

His patience in his constant pain,
  Content with humble lot;
His royal words of kindly cheer,
  His constant pining not,

Could but inspire me much, and drive

The last mind cloud away,

And radiance pour, and song call forth,

And blissful make the day.

How brightly danced a near cascade;

The birds sang overhead!

Joy ruled the hour! Faith cheered me on,

And Doubt, grim Doubt, was dead!

THE ACHIEVEMENT.

THE book was done, in pleasant verse
  On Smiths and other men ;
And when 'twas done you had a thought
  To write it through again.

The critics were considerate,
  Right well the volume took ;
Rich merchants sought to grasp your hand,
  Wise teachers liked the book.

A gunboat captain said, " Old boy,
  You have a prosperous gale ;
You're wise enough to shun the rocks,
  I'm proud to see you sail! "

Heaven bless the Hadley farmer

Who drove straight into town

And bought two copies of the book,

And laid his money down,

Remarking, " I delight to read

A book of home-like lays,

Rehearsing scenes of common life

In simple, lucid phrase;

" A volume penned by one who sees

A hero in a frock,

And likes to tell the praises of

Each mountain, rill and rock."

A book man whose most freezing words

So tortured you at first,

Who socially, and at his stand,

    Planned keen and did his worst

To crush your enterprise with sneers,

    Seemed quite another man,

When all his town had bought your book,

    And critics praised its plan.

Such greetings kind ; such rosy smiles !

    Such fawnings for your hand ;

Three several notes so humbly put,

    And signed, "Yours to command !"

An average aristocrat,

    Residing down at Ware,

Addressed a note that he was glad

    Your prospects were so fair.

Then you recalled how once he sneered,
    And now, to make amends,
He sought to join the numerous group
    Of your fair-weather friends.

Their sickly praise, so overdone,
    Showed hollowness of heart;
How much unlike the Squire's good words,
    "I'm proud to see you start."

And 'mid this meant and unmeant praise
    You kept a humble mind,
And sought in grander schemes and work
    Your joy and rest to find.

ANOTHER EXPERIENCE.

ABOUT the tender passion
  You had some luck unkind;
And yet in that deep sorrow
  Refreshing good you find.
It grieved her much to tell you,
  "Dear James, we now must part;
But you be good and noble
  And show a manly heart.

"I wish that I could wed you,
  But that may never be;
And, in the great hereafter,
  That I am true you'll see.

I'm going to teach a mission

    For cast-off girls and boys;

Therein is my ambition,

    And there I'll have my joys.

"I'll never wed another,

    And you are free to love;

Choose some delightful maiden;

    We three will meet above!"

You chose again, dear comrade,

    With wisdom in your choice;

And at the happy marriage

    Your friends had right rejoice.

The other one is busy

    Her mission field to keep,

But prays each day that angels

　Forbid you cause to weep.

Your wife is true and loving;

　You walk together well;

And noble things about her

　You always have to tell.

4

GOING TO GOTHAM.

ONCE on important business
    You drove to Gotham down,
At first all things went wrongly;
    It seemed a drear old town.
Each man you met was stubborn,
    No one could see like you;
And still you thought "in some way
    I'll fight this business through."

You left the city thinking
    The omens augured well;
And felt assured when passing
    The rocks at New Rochelle,

That brighter days were dawning,

    And you were on the track ;

With promise of good progress,

    And no more sliding back.

Although but little headway

    The train, at times, has made,

With scarce the power to forward

    The coaches up the grade;

You still have been advancing,

    Have reached the town at last,

With many friends to greet you,

    And skies of pleasant cast!

TWO PLACES.

FORGIVING my rejoinder—
    Dear friend, you paint a view
Of life's wed sweet and bitter,
    As it appeared to you?
For that it little matters;
    Your healthy words of cheer
Fill this auspicious morning
    With hopes forever dear.

True, James; near yours my birthplace,
    Where I may never be
And not desire to journey
    That place no more to see.
As there my noble parents

Had want and scornful laugh;
And there life's cup of bitter
My lips were forced to quaff.

But still the place was lovely;
Some people were quite kind;
The others I will pardon
When they may feel inclined.
It is not wise nor manly
To nurse our griefs too long;
Let's seek the pleasant parlor,
And hear the ladies' song.

We four, to-day, will journey,
So as to come in sight
Of that delightful village
Where you first saw the light;

Where winding hill-side roadways,

　　And purling, limpid streams,

Cool groves, and breezy hill-tops,

　　Excel our brightest dreams;

And where, abides a tanner,

　　A man urbane and true;

Who rose to estimation,

　　These western counties through;

The while his polished partner

　　Ruled well the Commonwealth,

Full careful of the treasures

　　And of the public health.

Although a central railway

　　Teems with its thundering trains,

The place is blest with quiet

As were Arcadian plains.

The psalmist had sung grander;

Inditing here his psalm,

And found for griefs and trouble

Sufficient grace and balm.

These scenes a Yankee school-girl

Has painted finely grand;

The woman should have praises

Throughout our Yankee land.

And here may still this artist

Depict the pleasant scene

Of rock, cascade, and forest,

And hillside dressed in green.

Arrived, we'll seek the dwelling

Of that kind-hearted man,

Who helped you to accomplish

Your dearly cherished plan.

With thanks for that first kindness

Which ever will be new,

Ours be a hearty promise

To fight life's battle through.

"WHERE PLEASANT PEOPLE TARRY."

MISCELLANEOUS.

ON CANTERBURY GREEN.*

THROUGHOUT the land, from east to west,
   No more inviting scene,
Along the streams, and on the plains,
   And all the hills between,
Than cheers the hearts of country folk
   On Canterbury Green,

When summer sunset mellowness
   Rests kindly on the place,
And tired toilers, from the fields,
   Their homeward journey trace ;
And, at the evening meal, glad hearts
   Devoutly utter grace.

* Canterbury, Ct.

The little smithy blazes still,

 The "great" elm tree is nigh, .

Rock maples shade the "Blackhill" road,

 The Quinneboag floats by ;

And citizens for factories

 Still unsuccessful try.

The score of dwellings are the same

 As in the days of yore ;

The school is undeserted yet,

 The all important "store"

Holds still the post, and gossips there

 Still tell their stories o'er.

There calico, and crockery,

 And picture-books are seen,

And ribbons still are sold, to deck

The girls of sweet sixteen,
And candy red, to please the boys
Of Canterbury Green.

Although the "training days" are gone,
And husking bees are few,
And old-time ways of dress and calls
Have given place to new,
And many faces known of yore
Are sleeping 'neath the yew,

Good people still inhabit here,
And thrift and peace are seen,
As when, a hundred years ago,
The pioneers, I ween,
Broke turf on old Westminster hill
And Canterbury Green.

The people yet are well aware
  What ancient " meetings " mean ;
The order is two sermons now,
  With " nooning " wedged between,
Within the church that still remains
  On Canterbury Green.

And where the neighbors worship yet
  On good Westminster hill,
The old style gospel preaching lasts,
  The ancient singing still:
And much we hope, in future years,
  This service ever will.

In spite of all, there lingers still,
  And ever will be seen,
A *shade* at which " all hands " were scared

And showed their foolish spleen,

Famed Prudence Crandall's colored school,

   On Canterbury Green.

Far back in eighteen thirty-three,

   Town meetings fierce were seen

Within the galleries of the church

   On· Canterbury Green ;

And speeches, A. T. Judson made,

   Complete, close put, and keen,

Against importing negroes there,

   To learn to read and spell :

That were unchristian and unwise,

   In no case was it well ;

In fact, they all, by vote, agreed,

   The business smacked of hell.

Although the school was broken up,
　　The "cause" good progress made,
And now the Canterbury folk,
　　Of every name and grade,
Desire their parents' foolish ways
　　From memory to fade.

But last it will, that colored fuss
　　Of eighteen thirty-three ;
And yet we'll think that good may still
　　At Canterbury be ;
And thank the Lord that colored folks
　　Throughout the land are free.

In other towns much foolishness
　　And inconvenient spleen,
And other pale folks to the blacks

Behaved as small and mean,

As they who spoiled the colored school

On Canterbury Green.

While Yankee Doodle is our song,

And stars and stripes are seen,

May Canterbury folk have peace,

And keep their record clean,

And everybody speak good words

Of Canterbury Green.

"BRIGHT IN A PEACEFUL VALLEY."

BRIGHT in a peaceful valley
   A happy village sweet,*
Where homes of joy are ranged along
   A maple shaded street.

There dwells a manly merchant
   Who kindly deigned to feed,
And gave a cordial, friendly word
   To stranger man in need,

When through Otsego county,
   Within the Empire State,

* Worcester, N. Y.

All tired, disconsolate and faint,

 He came one autumn late.

He tells to me his story

 And asks that I rehearse,

The deed and his felt gratitude;

 But I have not the verse

To paint aright the village,

 Within the Empire State,

Wherein this manly neighbor dwells

 Whose kindness makes him great.

CLARK AND THE TWENTY-FIRST.

WHEN Colonel Clark of Amherst
Was major in the field,
Contending in the Southland
To make the rebels yield,
The general said, "Brave major,
You and the Twenty-first
Must charge the rebels yonder,
Where they will do their worst."

Then prompt the major uttered
The simple answer, "Yes!"
And bravely they moved forward
Whom we delight to bless.

And there, upon famed Roanoke,

   Clark and the Twenty-first

Discomfited the rebels,

   Who did their bitter worst.

And in the rebel stronghold

   The Bay State flag was placed,

And bright a starry banner

   The rebel fortress graced.

And through much more of fighting

   Clark and his men were true ;

They went forth strong a thousand,

   They came a war-worn few !

The angels kept the leader

   Who dared the thickest fight,

And fought to hold the colors .

And keep our honor bright.

Then much the rebels hated,

And often since have cursed,

Whom we delight to honor,

Clark and the Twenty-first.

God bless all gallant soldiers

Who battled for the flag,

And aided in the conquest

Of Davis, Lee, and Bragg.

And, through our glorious future,

A song to all who erst

In bravery resembled

Clark and the Twenty-first!

THREE FRIENDS.

THESE lines to three devoted friends
    Whom I can not forget,
In all the ups and downs of life,
    Till life's last sun shall set:

The probate judge at Franklin's shire,
    A man of grace and grit,
Who, by his learning and his worth
    Is for his station fit;

A tall, strong miller, wise, and built
    With sunshine in his heart,

Residing in South Hadley, near

A pleasant school of art;

A Lisbon man whose greeting kind

Transforms New York, to me,

From busy Babel to a place

Of fountain, flower and tree.

The Lord have pity on the man

Who scorns to have a friend;

How high his plans, at last they must

In bad disaster end.

Napoleonic men may fight

Their battles all alone,

But finally a Waterloo

Their rashness will atone.

Lord grant I learn the useful fact,

    We are by others strong;

And they sing sweetest who have heard

    Another sing the song.

ON A TWENTIETH ANNIVERSARY.

TWO decades bright with blessings since
    We 'gan life's road together,
And each to other promised faith
    In every sort of weather.

With gratitude and joyfulness
    At good with which He crowned us,
We look unto the Father high,
    And thank the friends around us.

And here with them we offer prayers
    That through each coming season
Our friends and we abundantly
    Be blest with health and reason.

.

And, that we have great things to say,

  We're minded first and chiefly,

The words that speak and reach the heart

  Are spoken plain and briefly.

"TOO MANY HEARTS ARE SAD TO-NIGHT."

TOO many hearts are sad to-night,
I may not dance to music light.
They're sad from hunger and from pain,
And sad from sin's polluting stain.
Low down in cellars, up the stairs,
Where freely pass the winter airs ;
'Neath wretched shed, and in the street,
Where pelt the piercing storms of sleet,
Are pallid cheek, and sunken eyes,
And forms that never more may rise.
I may not dance to music light,
Too many hearts are sad to-night.
But some will wake, if touched aright,
To noble purpose and brave deed,

And grandly with their duty speed,

Achieving full, complete success,

While all the world, admiring, bless.

All this, if, now, one word, aright,

While you may skip to music light,

I speak to cheer them for the fight.

Too many hearts are sad to-night;

I may not dance to music light.

"FROM SUCH AS THESE, GOOD LORD."

FROM up-start mayors of little towns,
  With vanity inflated,
Whose worth, by citizens and self,
  Is vastly overrated;

From wordy politicians, bent
  On making a sensation;
From new-made agents of the mills
  Who don't deserve the station;

From officers who went to war
  To dangle swords about 'em,
And· eyed the enemy from far,
  But never tried to rout 'em;

Who drew revolvers on their men,

    To bring complete submission,

But ne'er before the foe assumed

    Belligerent position ;

From dapper " profs " in charge of schools

    Demanding able teachers ;

From puppet pulpiters, in place

    Of royal men, for preachers ;

From consequential merchants, proud

    Of " our superior dry goods ;"

From those who visit stores to look,

    But never go to buy goods ;

From men who visit editors

    To teach them journalism,

6

Or pelt some rival citizen,

Or air some social schism;

From men imbued with sham reforms,

A howling round the cities;

From other mobilier fuss,

Or mobilier committees;

From men who prove supremely small

When you expect them royal;

From citizens who traitors turn,

When they are expected loyal—

From such as these, good Lord, defend,

And graciously deliver,

And send us manly men instead,

And we will praise thee ever.

But since at home we're highly blest

    And of such plagues divested,

I'll say by incidents afar

    These verses were suggested.

And, while we pray that Heaven may grant

    We have. such ·curses never,

We'll pity people cursed with them

    In places——down the river !

A SUNDAY AT BUFFALO.

IF ever a mortal was worn,
   I found myself so by the lake,
The very best object on earth
   On which funny verses to make.

Then luckily thought came of one
   Who gladly would show me his home,
And deem me unkind not to call,
   And happiness find to say, come.

By him I was rested and fed
   And treated to many good rhymes,

Preserved in a scrap book, to keep

Remembrance of old Yankee times.

On Sunday we called at a church

Where trim a sleek preacher stood up

And talked his pink nothings so soft,

I prayed the good Lord he would stop!

Or turn his attention to hell,

Say bad men were going straight there,

And every one needed to mourn,

And give himself up unto prayer.

'Twere better than bass-wood and soap

And soft sighs of sweetness so fine,

Which the "ton" in their ecstacy said,

Were "thplendid, and gwand, and diwine!"

On Monday the "zephyrs" blew bleak

And cheerfully howled from the lake,

As forth in good season I drove,

The 'Lantic express train to take.

WORDS TO MY WIFE.

DEAR wife : amid the work that comes
   My absence to prolong,
I take this bright and sunny hour
   To rhyme for thee a song,

And thank thee for thy earnest prayers,
   That God hath answered well,
In health, and hope, and many joys,
   I have not time to tell ;

In friends who cheer me at my tasks,
   And pray that God will bless,
And earnestly and constantly
   Desire me good success ;

In grit to work and to endure,
   And for success to wait ;
In faith that God will keep me safe
   From every cruel fate ;

In faith that God is always thine,
   And sends his angels near,
To guard and guide the darling one
   Who holds my interests dear.

Pittsfield, September, 1873.

A MAN OF PROVIDENCE.

TO REV. E. F. C.

IN Providence a man so kind, so good,

   So wise, the city seemed correctly named;

A man who copied well John Wesley's life,

And Christ the heavenly master followed well,

And honored well an ancient order, grand

With many quiet men, who much have done

To banish want, and light this darkened world;

A man whose heavenly business did not bar

From frequent trips to glens and breezy hills;

A man whose luck with rod and line on lake

And brook, far up the pleasant Pine Tree State,

Was known and liked by all his happy flock.

Would there were more like him to bless the world,

And change, or crowd from foothold here below,

The men who so embitter earth by self,

And doubt of other men, and hate at sight

Of their aspiring looks and skyward steps,

That earth which should be heaven hath very hell

Wherever their drear, bitter, presence bad

Is permanent.

THE "RIVER ROAD." *

IN joyous spring or winter cold,
    And in the autumn sun,
The trains upon our northern route
    With good success are run.

And, bound to Methodistic camp,
    Or going mountainward,
On picnics bent, or politics,
    The people with accord

Declare they like the "River Road,"
    Its managers and men ;
And when they wish another ride,
    They'll try that route again.

*Connecticut River Railroad.

THE ALLOPATHS.

I WISH that all the allopaths
  Had all their sins forgiven,
And were translated from the earth
  To highest seats in heaven!

And all their books of medicine,
  And all the drugs they mix
Were ferried far, and finally,
  Beyond the river Styx!

The pleasant herbs that healthful grow
  On every happy hill,
God has ordained to aid the sick,
  And calomel will kill.

May light be given with coming years,

    And mild " botanics " rule ;

And only history record,

    There was another school !

www.ingramcontent.com/pod-product-compliance
Lightning Source LLC
Chambersburg PA
CBHW020029030726
47499CB00007B/2346